Praise for
Naming a Dying Thing

"In Vic Nogay's *Naming a Dying Thing*, time is like the shiny globe sitting on the teacher's desk; one can choose to handle it carefully, or one can choose to spin it wildly. Nogay takes time in her hands and sends it careening through moments sticky with loss. These moments of grief are coordinates, the points by which we make sense of direction, how we know if we're moving forward, backward, or nowhere at all. Nogay plots the familiar path of womanhood—heartbreak, sacrifice, self-neglect—and repackages them in brief and brutal snapshots. Readers will be unmoored from their own present, dropped into their own ugly moments. And Nogay makes sure we have language for the dead when we arrive at their graves."

Taylor Byas, author of *I Done Clicked My Heels Three Times* and *Resting Bitch Face*

~

"The poems in Vic Nogay's new collection *Naming a Dying Thing* are haunted and haunting. While the ghostly voices of past Ohio poets echo throughout these poems (Mary Oliver, James Wright, and Kenneth Patchen, come to mind), Nogay is able to—through the alchemy of her exceptional talent as a writer—conjure a distinctly unique and powerful poetic voice that is all her own. Throughout this collection, Nogay tackles complex paradoxes, such as nature and technology, serenity and violence, personal choice and societal pressures. But Nogay's keen eye for detail ("the wind waves / turkey foot & nodding rye / in hushing comfort") works as a kind of landmark-based navigation that allows her—and her readers—to travel through a chaotic world without ever feeling lost. In the end, Nogay's poems will haunt you in all the best ways, like the voice of a long-lost loved one you hear whenever you see something beautiful that reminds you of them."

Kip Knott, author of *The Other Side of Who I Am*, *Clean Coal Burn*, and *Tragedy, Ecstasy, Doom, and so on*

"*Naming a Dying Thing* by Vic Nogay is a collection of words and poems calling something forth from the wilderness in all of us. In her opening synopsis, she describes how mothers and women are expected to be nothing and everything at once. These poems reiterate over and over: there is strength in softness, a need to be seen and heard, not for show but for the spirit we encapsulate beneath our skin. In her poem, "birds are singing in december when you say that you are leaving me," [she writes] "ten thousand tiny bird wings / out of my mouth," [creating] a familiarity of raw ache calling from those forbidden depths of our hearts. Hear me, I am woman, the soil beneath our feet gives birth to our pain, our want can be found sewn in between the lines of each of these poems. Life is evident in these haunting revelations."

Sage Ravenwood, author of *Everything That Hurt Us Becomes a Ghost*

~

"These are urgent poems of witness: to birth, to death, and to the rough work that comes of living. With rural splendor and stark, quiet beauty, Vic Nogay chronicles the collapse. And what we make of what's next. "[N]ight will hold us," she writes, "if the earth will / tuck us in." In her midnight wisdom, Nogay implores us to stop, to see if the tears we've planted have grown wings. This is the voice of hardscrabble prophecy, a spirit of the night who will leave the light on."

Alison Stine, author of *Dust, Trashlands,* and *Road Out of Winter*

~

"Vic Nogay leads us through *Naming a Dying Thing*, where Ohio's wilderness becomes the lens for her exploration of womanhood. I found myself nodding in agreement with my own journey as a woman, partner, and mother. I felt connected to the struggles and wonder we share across differences. All the seasons of life here, all the heavy truths unflinching. These lovely poems reveal what it costs to hold the beauty and the breaking."

Amy Turn Sharp, poet and artist

Naming a Dying Thing

by
Vic Nogay

YELLOW ARROW
PUBLISHING
Baltimore, Maryland, USA

Naming a Dying Thing
Copyright © 2025 by Yellow Arrow Publishing
All rights reserved.

Library of Congress Control Number: 2025946544
ISBN (paperback): 979-8-9883176-8-5

Cover art and design and interior art by Alexa Laharty
(Instagram @alexaelisabeth).
Interior design by Yellow Arrow Publishing.
For more information, see yellowarrowpublishing.com.

For every mother and every daughter
(but especially Nelle, Wenny, and Pax)

Contents

NAMING A DYING THING

Nursing by the window on a red dawn

Two vultures helm
the meadow's poles;
a row among the rest
for first mate.

Twin fawns asunder,
the wind waves
turkey foot & nodding rye
in hushing comfort.

A nearby doe calls,
then listens.

Testimony

A witness of my miscarriage, for Brittany Watts

At ten weeks, for six days, I labored;
my body exiled my body.

When it was over, I did not look
but let my love hallow

our hands in the stagnant fruit,
the cardinal leavings.

We bound a clot with cloth
and thyme and earthed it

between the ancient roots of the sugar maple
and the fruitless, shallow juniper.

> *I flushed the rest.*
> *What else was I to do?*

Becoming is an unmade promise.
Dark red; blue seed; bruise.

Now you are six

cake sugar on cheeks, hair sun-dried,
sweat-frosted from late summer,
my ear to your back, you fall asleep.

I'm holding you and my breath
while your big bluestem heart beats
under thunder and a sturgeon moon.

dark shrouds your drowsing creek bed eyes.
high midnight clouds hide steady stars.
I dare not wish on what I cannot see.

The Great Girl Evaporation of 2022

In February, the creek flooded the fields forty yards on either side
from the tracks to the freeway. That was the last of the rain.

The men in charge set the burn ban in June, but that didn't stop
them from striking us like matchsticks in the dry beds.
Our blood like a fresh, wet spring.

Our prayers cracked the corners of our mouths as a sheen of dust
settled in September. The burn ban held even as the nights grew
cold. We vaporized, hovered just above our bodies through the
fall, followed our husks like swollen clouds.

For all our prayers, heaven never answered. But something did.

The night we turned back the clocks, a dark disc descended.
The sky lit up like a million suns. A theft, or a mercy? It culled us,
body and soul, up, up with the water.

While the hawk preys

In heavy March,
railroad tracks and rural routes
cut Ohio deep—

frozen, empty
fields of soy and corn
sectioned off into a measured grid,

tracks and roads, straight and slim
like stitches closing
the white world, waiting.

This is not sweet June's
patchwork quilt,
not a honeysuckle breeze,

this is cars and trucks,
telephone lines,
the sick bite of sunlight

gasping, setting low
beneath the cloud bank, and you,
stopped at a train a mile long, waiting and waiting and waiting.

Folk tale

Every year
when it snows, a blushing
stain of berry juice grows
beneath American holly

behind the shed at the
back of our lot
just before the meadow
dives into rugged, wooded

rocks and fallen limbs,
down to the creek where
frogs and flies and birds play
murder in the summer. In winter,

the holly hosts one white squirrel—
niveous and ghost-like.
Berry droppings from his fêtes
dot the bleached earth.

—

They wouldn't let me take the body,
born before I even knew, so I
burned my clothes and buried the ash
beneath the holly before the ground froze.

When the snow melts,
the berries hallow the earth;
I check the spot every spring to see
if there's a baby growing from the ground.

i dream of the deer /
in marriage counseling

i tuck my body
into where the tree line
breaks. you hide

far behind, not seeing
me in the midday dark
of old growth.

deer clear me
as if i were brush,
turn back and suckle

the palms of my hands;
their tongues deterge
my eyes, my ears.

big bodies
light as light
until felled.

you rise
and blow the smoke
from your gun.

/

you laugh at
this part, say,
that's not how it works,

but when i say again,
i dream of the deer,
your set mouth turns down,

your hard eyes turn downy,
blinking back tears,
your calloused chest exhales

a firm rebuke,
and sow thistle
burrows out of me.

Sunk cost

The decanter suffers
the fight, breaks—
a piece of glass finds

the soft inside
of my arm,
and I leave it.

When it snows

What I remember most is how the subzero night turned your
fur to shattering needles that poked holes in my gloves as I
wrenched you from the doghouse floor, and how your body—I
had to literally break it to get it free—sounded just like anything
else frozen, like leaves unraked in a sudden October snow,
crystallized, splintering under my boot, or a shovel on a sidewalk,
or an ice machine, or a . . . before I moved you, I took your
picture for evidence; you were lying on your side as if sleeping,
as if you hadn't suffered although I knew you had, and you
reminded me of the boy I knew in school who left my room one
night in January, steamy and stumbling the wrong way home
after a kiss, in the doorway, so wet my face froze when he pulled
away, and when he never texted, I went out looking until I found
him the next morning curled up in the snow under a shimmering
pine tree, as if he hadn't suffered either.

stillborn

september sunlight seems
a sadness, this darkness
is the clear view.
if this quiet
night will hold us,
if the earth will
tuck us in, together
may we regrow
perennial
come spring.

Kindergarten Graduation

Memorial Day 2022, after Uvalde

a flag crouches, quiet
small, in shadow
behind the singing bodies of our babies

my daughter stands
body to body on chorus risers
the pink puff sleeves of her

favorite dress reach out
and rest on the shoulders
of someone else's children

Swan Lake

I do wonder / at all the ways men spit / into nature's current—
mow down a forest / to build two hundred houses, all / alike,
predictable, safe, / then plant trees down every street / and leave
space for a little park / make sure to build a pond for the view, for
the brochure, / but don't let any ducks or geese come around / put
fake plastic / swans in the ponds / at the park to scare the geese
away / *don't those stupid birds know it's not for them*?

in the winter, the pond freezes / the hollow swans, trapped / in
the middle. sometimes / someone thinks they're real / gets scared
/ calls the cops / *please save them!* / *but then put them somewhere*
else or kill them for all I care / *they can't stay here* / *I can't have*
them / *shitting on my lawn.*

birds are singing in december
when you say that you are leaving me

i hold my rotted tongue
& hum to the lake
& the mirror of the moon.

i sketch my face in gray scale,
scale the gray rock face,
its cuts deep, catching on

the bubbled bell sleeves
of a certain dress—
let the hard rocks keep

that ivory muslin. torn,
i rage beneath tall pines & you
can cloak the heavy edges of the night

on me, steep
my knotted braids,
a fresh tangle of nested brush,

into fire.
light me up & listen
for the passerine,

furious & thrumming—
ten thousand tiny bird wings
out of my mouth.

Atropos, Goddess of Fate, Faces Her Own

After birth, you are so quiet on my chest. I am aglow. My head's a dizzy bliss. My heart's an ocean swell. Each cell is buzzed and humming, euphoric in a summer storm just before the lightning strike.

The midwife placed you here, your skin to my skin, and covered us with muslin. She wipes what's left of the womb off you, clears your ears and nose. I want to tell her to stop, that it's no use. I was never meant to be a mother. You are not my fate. But I'm addicted to this open moment when anything is possible, when I could dream of bringing life instead of bringing death.

And so, I dream. I watch her at her work. Her sacred, hopeless work. I try to nurse you, but you won't. Your mouth, wet and slack, is too lost to latch. Your tongue flickers gently in vain.

My sisters fill the farthest corner of the room like shadows, waiting for their time. They know I can't do this on my own. For now, the cord is still pulsing—one life becoming two. But soon the flow will stem, and our roseate bond will pale. I have always known how it would end.

So here we are together, so few moments left. Both of us now barely breathing. Your chest trips in weak attempts. Mine catches in time with yours—a primal prayer.

I cup the soft shell of your head in my palm and will your eyes to open, to see me, just one time. *Wake up*, I whisper, smiling through a sob. Your eyelids twitch. Unlit suns knead beneath them, and it looks like you are dreaming, like you are searching the dark for me.

The shadows shift as my sisters make their way to me. The saturnine hush and sweep of their skirts spark a panic at the base of my throat—a bird's winged beating against the backs of clamped teeth. My eyes pour beseeching tears.

Bedside now, my sisters' sighs quiver a wisp of your hair. My frantic eyes meet theirs. They clasp my hand, and it rises like a marionette's. I cocoon myself around you and disgorge a withered howl.

They measure your thread with solemn eyes and weave my fingers into the shears.

Milk

Loamy wetland,
winter melt, flood-
plain after fatal April.
I am sour with the weight.

Late summer with a lover by a man-made pond

Pond algae bloats, overfed and merciless. Mosquitoes reign where fatheads sour, their rotting bodies gather and release, grease-slick at the surface of this olid basin. My lover boors, *Summer is dead.* As I plead my dissent, *See the dragonflies? How they mate in midair? How she spirals and hooks her body for him* . . . the portentous decay of phantoms out of fish bodies congests my heart inside my throat.

Suddenly repulsed, she freezes, faking her own death in revolt. But in this false idyll, these discordant loves find putrescent ends. She hits the water in gravid protest, dying anyway.

No point in keeping secrets

If I could rewrite that night I spent with you in the woods
somewhere in the Appalachian foothills, in a summer so hot
the earth wheezed when the sun went down and steam pooled
above the blacktop making rivers of the air, I would give in
to you running your cool fingers up and down my bare arms,
give in to your mouth on my inner thigh, give in to us, just
kids, trying . . . I'll always wish you'd've given in first so I could
have made you feel my body ringing beneath the surface of my
skin, quaking the roots of the tree where we slept, shaking the
buckeyes loose from above, ushering in low rumbles from a
distant storm, my ears swelling and blistering while you sang into
my open mouth, too hot to hear a thing.

Even if I burn

If you could reach inside my body
through the pupils of my eyes that open
and close to the light like windows, I would open

for you, tear down the blinds, blind
my eyes in the morning sun so you could see,
so you could climb inside, touch

my memories with your fingertips,
pull them out, set them free,
hang each one,

deftly, on the low limbs
of an oak in the summer
by the river to bleach out in the sun.

A toad perched on a rock
by the water and a dove swimming
in the leaves of the tree will pretend

not to watch
you leaf through me
like a sacred relic.

There will be no
museum or sterile box
for these.

Shade the trees with memory,
honor me with sun-
light—even if I burn.

a place

a place by the canal sells frozen custard.
you sit in an old canoe,
washed ashore decades before,
and lick your drips
while cicadas sing
and fireflies hang in the humidity—
a summer snow globe.

you've heard the stories of the kids who've fallen in,
and you're careful not to be reckless,
but some days you inch down
the concrete wall to find them.
you shed your shoes and rest
just the soles of your bare feet
on the surface of the water,
and call,
like magnets,
the pieces of their bodies logged in water's memory
to you.

when someone asks you cheekily, *do you believe in ghosts?*
you flinch because you do.

My daughter builds a deathbed for the bug in the bay window

Four blooms from the trillium,
two from the common rue,
rotting refuse from the peace
lily that never quite recovered
from our cross-country move.

A deflated grape, white with mold,
performs as treacly stand-in
'til she sanctifies the scene
with a perimeter of bread crust—a magic circle.

I need not ask if she saw
the fluid on my floral sheets
or the shape of my arms around them
or what I bedded down and buried
in the old yard.

I listen, still, for the sound of the train in the summer

under an august full moon, we looked like spirits in the night—
fuzzy, formless to any watching eyes. our bodies lingered after
themselves like smoke in the wind, a gossamer brushstroke.
constellations hooked their skeleton arms into the road-worn
hems of our once-white skirts, lacing us into the goldenrod and
aster, graying in the dark.

when we reached the train, we stood back from the tracks,
paused to watch metal in motion. the force of it repelled us like
antigravity—we fell into the weeds, tumbling with the bugs.
supine, holding hands, we listened to the reverb of the train, of
the song, of the summer, of the end.

and still we listened
for what's sacred in the dark
once all'd gone quiet.

&

a daughter is the runaway
a mother is the rope
& the runaway

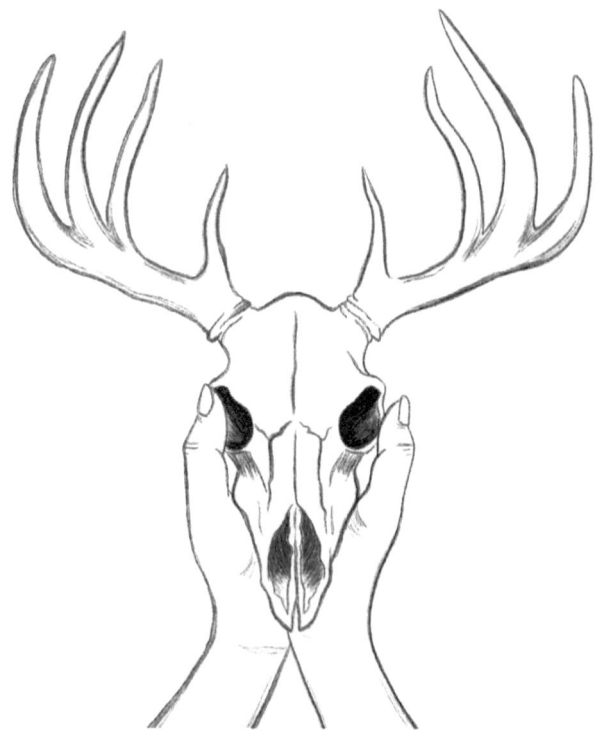

women

up the hill lived an old woman.
our backyards collided.
where the grass should have been,
just high, dry weeds.
the roof caved above the porch
shading unwashed windows shrugging off their shutters.
"posted: no trespassing" posted everywhere.

on a day when a bravery possessed me,
I climbed the hill.
I found a deer skull in a shed,
and I held it like a kindred spirit.
proof of death made life in me,
turned bravery to wicked wildness.

no, it couldn't be a woman who lived there.
from all the nonfiction my mother buried in performance,
I learned women keep up appearances.
and all that wildness is a secret.

Paraphyly

What I mean when I say,
>*don't be afraid of the bees,*

is that I can't take one more fear—
I have enough of my own
that I've packed up neat in boxes
with bows to bury and forget.
>*Let no one unbury them.*

If, one day, when you're grown
and moving through the world,
you find yourself moving like me,
like I moved like my mother,
like she moved like hers,
bury your fears in the yard with mine.
>*Why is fear what we pass down?*

What I mean is,
>*please don't keep our fears with you.*

We have buried them deep beneath
the earth to soften your step.
What I mean is,
>*let us soften.*

What I mean is,
>*we don't need to be hard to be strong.*

New Physics

I used to ride the swings,
summers at the county fair.
My mother on the bench
by the cotton candy stand
could not watch my body,
a limb from her body,
whirl through the air—
a universe in a bucket seat, held
by rust-flaked chains
and a whip of loose nylon.
Back behind our home, my daughter
floats from the pin oak—
her rainbow saucer swing
a perfect circle
beneath the ess of her
arms and lengths of hair
loosing from yesterday's plaits.
I no longer have the heart for spinning things.
That nylon strap,
that weathered branch
broke with the water.
She blurs before my eyes,
asks, heady, through a glorying grin,
if the sky has started turning,
and the earth is standing still.

the revivals we cleave, we endure

when she came to me at dawn / i was already spinning in the water up to my ankles with my long cotton cardigan pulling wet and winding up around my knees / body nude but glitter-sparking in the summer sun / there were mothers and sons and grandmas with their dogs and husbands walking by and looking without looking / and some even looked / like really looked / but i couldn't be moved by any force but my own / my arms open wide while the world renamed me Beautiful because i was alive / and coming alive again.

when i came home near noon / light and heavy and sparkling new / i shed golden champagne skin of the morning around carelessly in the garden and on the sun-kissed heads of my children so they would grow roots and grow strong and grow real and irrefutable / i left some in our bed and painted it on my reflection in the mirror so i could see it when i didn't believe / i sent some through the air vents and down drains so it would travel far and maybe come back to me too / someday / when i might need it.

when you woke at dusk some nights later / you thundered / unhinged the sky into your orbit / in the rain / you opened your mouth to let the water soothe the blackouts stuck to your teeth / cavities or carbon or the colossal crack of gunfire // you choked / forked a single speck of glitter from under your tongue / and spit it out at your feet.

Appalachians

After Maggie Smith

I am not your child, though I have longed for you.
From the left-behind plateau, I have watched the once-

swollen shadow of you, beyond sun-bright, red-capped
fingertips even on the longest days. I know your hills

are a small bump, emptying, cowing to the weight
of loss, of naming a dying thing.

I am trying to find wonder in the world, but I have
driven many highways, seen you flayed, our names

in paint, sprayed and slipping down the length of you.
Rock cuts weep at earliest light, and the sun tries to make you

a miracle. It's too late to turn this into something good,
to write a new beginning. Let's see this ending through.

You can call me orphan; I'll call you bereaved.
Rest now. You need not claim me.

Acknowledgments

Anti-Heroin Chic (online), October 2020
"women"

perhappened (online), December 2020
"When it snows"

Little Engines, March 2021
"Swan Lake" (as "Swan Lake, 2020")

Crow & Cross Keys (online), May 2021
"a place"

Lost Balloon (online), May 2021
"the revivals we cleave, we endure"

Capsule Stories, June 2021
"i listen, still, for the sound of the train in the summer"
"no point in keeping secrets"

Barren Magazine (online), March 2022
"Folk tale"

Gordon Square Review (online), May 2022
"i dream of the deer / in marriage counseling"

Olney Magazine, Kiss Your Darlings Anthology, August 2022
"birds are singing in december when you say
that you are leaving me"

ONE ART (online), June 2023
"While the hawk preys"

Stone Circle Review (online), August 2023
"even if i burn"

BRAWL (online), August 2024
"Kindergarten Graduation"
"New Physics"

Gone Lawn (online), August 2024
"Late summer with a lover by a man-made pond"

tiny wren lit (online), August 2024
"stillborn"

Tiny Molecules (online), October 2024
"Atropos, Goddess of Fate, Faces Her Own"

Lost Balloon (online), June 2025
"The Great Girl Evaporation of 2022"

Thank you to Madeline Anthes for inspiring me and encouraging me to return to the page.

Thank you to Claire Taylor for reading numerous early drafts of these pieces; your attention and thoughtful feedback are invaluable to me.

Thank you to Kelly Larkin for championing me.

Thank you to Mary and Neil Collins for being proud of me.

Thank you to all the editors who first published many of these pieces in their beautiful literary magazines.

Thank you to Yellow Arrow Publishing for publishing *Naming a Dying Thing*—a dream come true!

Thank you to my girls for your love and adoration.

Thank you to Stas for seeing me.

And thank You for holding this book in your hands.

VIC NOGAY is a Pushcart Prize and Best Microfiction nominated writer from Ohio. Her work has been published in *Gone Lawn*, *Tiny Molecules*, *Fractured Lit*, *Lost Balloon*, and other journals. She is the author of the micropoetry chapbook *under fire under water* (tiny wren, 2022) and is the microeditor of *Identity Theory*. Find her online @vicnogaywrites or haunting rural roadsides where the wildflowers grow.

Thank you for supporting independent publishing.

Yellow Arrow Publishing is a nonprofit supporting writers and artists who identify as women. Visit YellowArrowPublishing.com for information on our publications, workshops, and writing opportunities.